VICTORIAN EPICURE

Chocolate Lovers

Recipe Book

Livre de recettes pour les Mordus du Chocolat

Tel: (250) 385-6563
Fax: (250) 385-4558
E-Mail: hq@epicureselections.com
Web Site: www.epicureselections.com

Title: **Victorian Epicure Chocolate Lovers Recipe Book / Livre de recettes pour les mordus du chocolat**

Includes Index.

Cover design: Gillian Simpson

Victorian Epicure Inc.
Box 5700
Victoria, BC V8R 6S8

Printed and produced in British Columbia, Canada

First printing January 2001

Special Thanks

Our most special thanks to our customers, consultants and friends who have contributed recipes, tips and ideas for this book. We would also like to express our gratitude to Victorian Epicure Chef, Cheryl Warwick, who scrutinized the recipes for simplicity and clarity.

Table of Contents

Victorian Epicure Belgian Chocolate & Pure Cocoa Facts & Information

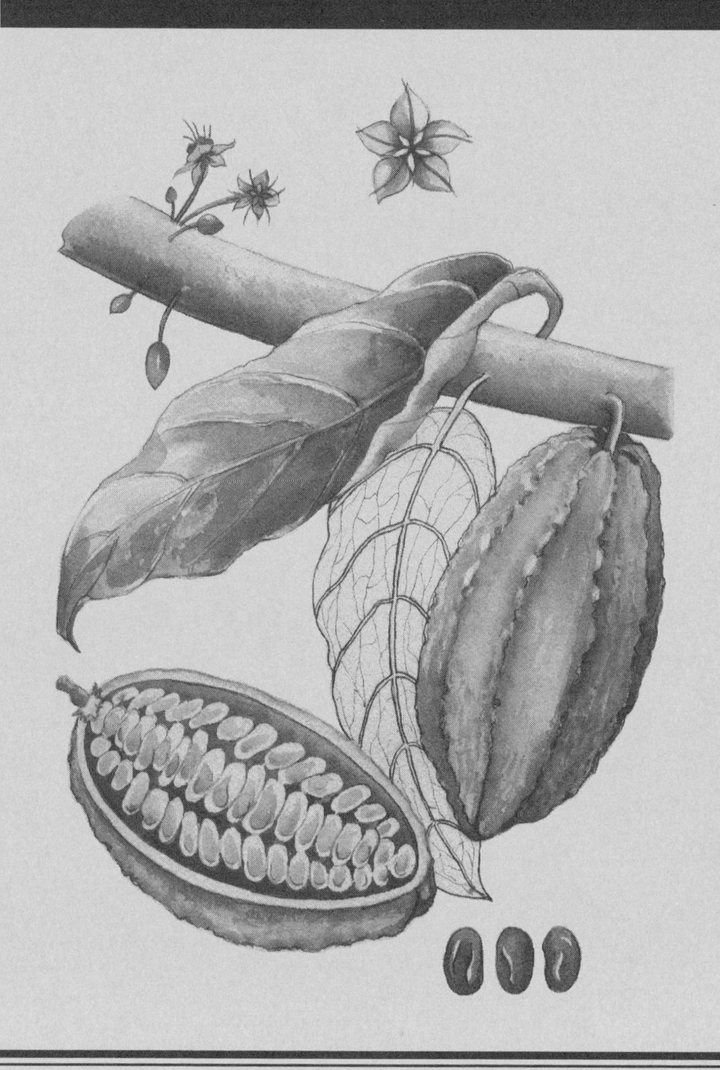

Victorian Epicure Pure Cocoa

Pure Cocoa is made from the dried paste that remains after cocoa butter (also known as chocolate liquor) has been removed during the production of pure chocolate. This paste is dried into a hardened mass that is ground into the powder that we know as cocoa.

The cocoa powder we have selected for Victorian Epicure is of premium quality with the highest percentage of cocoa butter. Regular cocoa powder contains between 10 and 22% cocoa butter and the Pure Cocoa we have selected has between 22 and 24%. Our VE Pure Cocoa is the darkest and richest available. Its velvety, smooth texture allows it to be easily blended with either liquid or dry ingredients.

Substituting Pure Cocoa for pure chocolate

1 oz unsweetened chocolate	=	3 Tbsp VE Pure Cocoa + 1 Tbsp butter
1 oz semi-sweet chocolate	=	3 Tbsp VE Pure Cocoa + 1 Tbsp butter + 1 Tbsp white sugar

Chocolate Facts and Information

Chocolate must always be stored in a cool, dry place. Chocolate can be kept indefinitely if stored properly. You will sometimes notice a slight white (or grey) coating on chocolate. This is called a bloom and it is a result of cocoa butter that has come to the surface. This bloom will disappear when melted or added to baking and it will, in no way, affect the fine taste or quality of chocolate.

SUCCESSFULLY MELTING CHOCOLATE

The fine chocolate that we have selected for VE is the best Belgian Chocolate. It is pure chocolate with a high cocoa butter content. It melts very smoothly and may be used wherever chocolate is needed. This "chip" form is very easy to measure, and its small size allows for quick, efficient melting. You will discover how easy it is to create beautifully dipped strawberries. The chocolate will set in a thin layer with a glossy finish.

The most important things to remember when melting chocolate is not to use excessive heat and to keep moisture of any kind away from the chocolate. Moisture is the enemy of chocolate!

Chocolate may be melted over direct heat when it is combined with other ingredients such as butter or cream. The mixture should be constantly stirred over low heat.

1. Always make sure your bowl is perfectly dry.
2. Use a double boiler for melting chocolate. Make sure the bowl you place on top of the hot (not boiling) water fits snugly so no steam will escape and possibly ruin your chocolate.
3. The best method is to bring 2" (5 cm) of water to a boil. Turn the heat off, then place the bowl of chocolate on top. There will be enough heat to melt the chocolate. Stir frequently, as the stirring action will promote faster melting.

Note: When melting chocolate keep the temperature below 120° F (48°C) (use Instant Read Thermometer)

Microwave Melting

It is possible to melt small amounts of chocolate in a microwave. You must be extremely diligent when using a microwave to melt chocolate. Chocolate is an expensive ingredient and must always be treated carefully in order to achieve best results. It is important to proceed slowly, 40 seconds at a time and stir often!

When melting chocolate in a microwave, the chocolate 'chips' will retain their original shape, so it is impossible to 'see' how it is melting, you must stir in order to monitor the melting process. Chocolate will continue to melt when stirred. If you do not stir chocolate while it is melting, the first pieces that melt will burn before the remaining chocolate is melted and this will ruin the entire batch.

Reminder: When melting chocolate keep the temperature below 120° F (48°C) (use Instant Read Thermometer).

Tips for Using Melted Chocolate

- Brush melted chocolate over the base of your favourite fruit tart or flan shells before filling - this will not only add a little chocolate flavour but will also prevent your pastry from getting soggy as the filling sits in the shell

- Drizzle melted chocolate over ice cream, over sponge or angel food cakes

- Drizzle or dip baked shortbread or sugar cookies

- Drizzle inside of dessert glasses before filling with mousse

Recipe Notes

1 oz chocolate	= 28 grams	= 2 Tbsp VE Belgian Chocolate
2 oz chocolate	= 56 grams	= 1/4 cup VE Belgian Chocolate
4 oz chocolate	= 112 grams	= 1/2 cup VE Belgian Chocolate
6 oz chocolate	= 168 grams	= 1 cup VE Belgian Chocolate

Correct Temperatures for Stages of Cooked Sugar

Note: Use a precice Candy Thermometer

Thread	215°F (102°C)
Pearl	220° to 222°F (104° to 106°C)
Soft Ball	234° to 242°F (112° to 116°C)
Firm Ball	244° to 248°F (118° to 120°C)
Hard Ball	250° to 266°F (121° to 130°C)
Soft Crack	270° to 290°F (132° to 143°C
Hard Crack	300° to 310°F (149° to 154°C)

Caramelized Sugar

Light Caramel	320° to 338°F (160° to 170°C)
Medium Caramel	356°F (180°C)
Dark Caramel	374°F (190°C)

COOKIES

1. VE Chocolate Chip Drop Cookies
2. Peanut Butter & Chocolate Chip Cookies
3. White Chocolate and Macadamia Nut Cookies
4. Chocolate Shortbread
5. Oatmeal and Chocolate Chip Cookies
6. Rum Balls
7. Soft Cocoa Cookies with White Chocolate Chips
8. Chocolate Shortbread Cookie Rolls
9. Chocolate Coconut 'Spiders'
10. Chocolate Chip Nut Cookies
11. Cocoa and Hazelnut Meringue Puffs

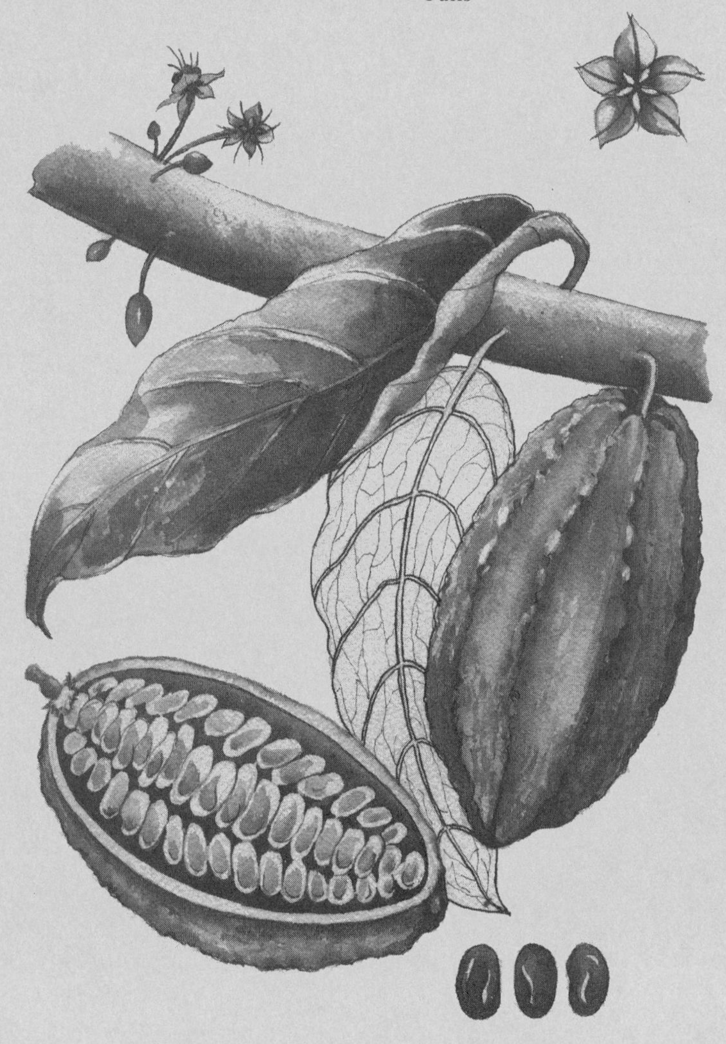

1. VE Chocolate Chip Drop Cookies

Makes 3 dozen

1/2 cup butter, at room temperature	**125 ml**
1/2 cup brown sugar	**125 ml**
1/2 cup white sugar	**125 ml**
1 egg	**1**
1 tsp VE Vanilla Extract	**5 ml**
1 cup flour plus 2 Tbsp all purpose flour	**280 ml**
1/2 tsp salt	**2.5 ml**
1/2 tsp baking soda	**2.5 ml**
1 cup VE Belgian Chocolate (Dark, Milk, or White)	**250 ml**

1. Preheat oven to 375°F (190°C).
2. Cream butter and both sugars. Add egg, VE Vanilla Extract and beat well.
3. Whisk together flour, baking soda and salt. Add to creamed mixture and beat until smooth.
4. Fold in VE Belgian Chocolate. Drop batter by spoon onto parchment lined bun pans, spaced well apart. Bake for 10 minutes or until lightly golden.

VE Vanilla Extract
VE Belgian Chocolate (Dark, Milk, or White)

2. PEANUT BUTTER & CHOCOLATE CHIP COOKIES

Makes 2 to 3 dozen

1/2 cup room temperature butter	**125 ml**
1/2 cup firmly packed brown sugar	**125 ml**
1/2 cup white sugar	**125 ml**
1 cup peanut butter	**250 ml**
1/2 tsp salt	**2.5 ml**
1 egg	**1**
1/2 tsp baking soda	**2.5 ml**
1 tsp VE Vanilla Extract	**5 ml**
1 to 1 1/2 cups flour (you will need the greater amount of flour if your peanut butter is heavy in oil)	**250-375 ml**
1 cup VE Belgian Dark or Milk Chocolate	**250 ml**

1. Preheat oven to 350°F (175°C).
2. Cream butter and both sugars. Add egg and beat well.
3. Beat in peanut butter, salt and VE Vanilla Extract.
4. Add flour and baking soda, beat until smooth. Add VE Belgian Chocolate.
5. Roll cookies into 1" (2.5 cm) balls, place on parchment lined bun pans. Press flat.
6. Bake for 10 to 12 minutes or until lightly golden.

VE Vanilla Extract
VE Belgian Dark or **Milk Chocolate**

3. WHITE CHOCOLATE AND MACADAMIA NUT COOKIES

Makes 2 to 3 dozen

1/2 cup butter	**125 ml**
1/2 cup brown sugar	**125 ml**
1/2 cup white sugar	**125 ml**
1 egg	**1**
1 tsp VE Vanilla Extract	**5 ml**
1 cup + 2 Tbsp all-purpose flour	**280 ml**
1/2 tsp salt	**2.5 ml**
1/2 tsp baking soda	**2.5 ml**
1/2 cup VE Belgian White Chocolate	**125 ml**
1/2 cup toasted, chopped macadamia nuts	**125 ml**

1. Preheat oven to 375°F (190°C).
2. Cream butter and both sugars. Add egg and VE Vanilla Extract.
3. Sift together flour, salt and baking soda. Add to creamed mixture and mix well.
4. Stir in VE Belgian White Chocolate and macadamia nuts.
5. Drop by spoonful onto parchment lined bun pan 2" (5 cm) apart. Bake for 10 minutes.

VE Vanilla Extract
VE Belgian White Chocolate

4. CHOCOLATE SHORTBREAD

Makes 3 dozen

1 cup cold butter, cut into small cubes	**250 ml**
1 1/2 cups all-purpose flour	**375 ml**
1 cup icing sugar	**250 ml**
1/3 cup VE Pure Cocoa	**80 ml**
1 tsp VE Vanilla Extract	**5 ml**

1. Preheat oven to 375°F (190°C).
2. Combine all ingredients in mixer or food processor until smooth.
3. Roll into a ball, flatten, wrap and chill for 15 minutes.
4. Roll out on lightly floured surface and cut into shapes. Place on parchment lined bun pans. Bake 8 to 10 minutes. Before serving dust lightly with VE Pure Cocoa or icing sugar using a dredger or a stainless steel strainer.

VE Pure Cocoa
VE Vanilla Extract

5. Oatmeal and Chocolate Chip Cookies

Makes 3 dozen

1/2 cup butter	**125 ml**
1/2 cup brown sugar	**125 ml**
1/2 cup white sugar	**125 ml**
1 egg	**1**
1 tsp milk	**5 ml**
1 tsp VE Vanilla Extract	**5 ml**
1/2 tsp baking soda	**2.5 ml**
1/2 tsp VE Baking Powder	**2.5 ml**
1/2 tsp salt	**2.5 ml**
1 cup rolled oats	**250 ml**
1 cup all-purpose flour	**250 ml**
3/4 cup VE Belgian Chocolate (Dark or Milk)	**180 ml**

1. Preheat oven to 350°F (175°C).
2. Cream butter and both sugars. Add egg, milk, VE Vanilla Extract and salt
3. Whisk together flour, baking soda, VE Baking Powder and rolled oats. Add to creamed mixture. When beaten smooth, add VE Belgian Chocolate Chips.
4. Drop cookies by teaspoon, 2" (5 cm) apart onto parchment lined bun pans.
5. Bake 10 to 12 minutes or until golden brown.

VE Vanilla Extract
VE Baking Powder
VE Belgian Chocolate (Dark or Milk)

6. Rum Balls

Makes about 3 dozen

1/2 cup VE Belgian Dark Chocolate, melted	**125 ml**
1/2 cup white sugar	**125 ml**
1/3 cup dark rum	**80 ml**
1/4 cup corn syrup	**60 ml**
2 tsp VE Cinnamon	**10 ml**
2 1/2 cups finely chocolate wafer crumbs	**625 ml**
3/4 cup finely chopped nuts	**180 ml**
VE Pure Cocoa, icing sugar or finely ground nuts for decorating*	

1. Melt chocolate in stainless steel bowl over hot water.
2. Mix in sugar, rum and syrup. Stir in chocolate wafer crumbs, VE Cinnamon and nuts. Mix thoroughly. Scrape down sides of bowl, cover and refrigerate until mixture is firm.
3. Form into 1" (2.5 cm) balls, roll in your choice or VE Pure Cocoa, icing sugar, ground nuts or chocolate wafer crumbs.
4. Layer in an airtight container, placing a sheet of parchment paper between the layers. Rum balls will keep for up to 1 month in the freezer.

*Note: This is an ideal recipe to double or triple. You can create 3 different types of rum balls, by rolling some in nuts, some in icing sugar and the remaining in VE Pure Cocoa.

VE Belgian Dark Chocolate
VE Cinnamon
VE Pure Cocoa

7. Soft Cocoa Cookies with VE Belgian White Chocolate

Makes 2 to 3 dozen

1/2 cup butter	**125 ml**
1 cup firmly packed brown sugar	**250 ml**
1/2 cup VE Pure Cocoa	**125 ml**
1 egg	**1**
2/3 cup milk	**160 ml**
1/4 tsp salt	**1.25 ml**
1 1/3 cup all-purpose flour	**330 ml**
1 Tbsp VE Baking Powder	**15 ml**
1 tsp VE Vanilla Extract	**5 ml**
2/3 cup VE Belgian White Chocolate	**160 ml**

1. Preheat oven to 375° F (190°C).
2. Cream butter and brown sugar. Add egg and VE Vanilla Extract and beat well.
3. Sift dry ingredients and add alternately with milk, mixing well after each addition.
4. Add VE Belgian White Chocolate. Drop by spoonful on parchment lined bun pans. Bake for 10 minutes.

VE Pure Cocoa
VE Baking Powder
VE Vanilla Extract
VE Belgian White Chocolate

8. CHOCOLATE SHORTBREAD COOKIE ROLLS

Makes 2 to 3 dozen

1 cup butter, at room temperature	**250 ml**
3/4 cup granulated sugar	**180 ml**
1 1/2 tsp VE Almond Extract	**7.5 ml**
1/4 cup VE Pure Cocoa	**60 ml**
2 tsp VE Baking Powder	**10 ml**
2 cups all-purpose flour	**500 ml**
1/2 cup VE Belgian White Chocolate, melted for dipping	**125 ml**

1. Cream butter and sugar until light and fluffy. Add VE Almond Extract and beat well.
2. Sift together VE Pure Cocoa, VE Baking Powder, and all-purpose flour.
3. Add to the creamed mixture and mix until dough forms.
4. Form into squared or triangular logs on parchment paper and roll up tightly. Refrigerate for at least 2 hours.
5. Preheat oven to 350°F (175ºC). Slice cookies 1/2" (1.25 cm) thick and place on parchment lined bun pans. Bake 10 minutes.
6. Drizzle or dip cookies in melted VE Belgian White Chocolate, let set until chocolate is firm.

VE Almond Extract
VE Pure Cocoa
VE Belgian White Chocolate
VE Baking Powder

9. CHOCOLATE COCONUT 'SPIDERS'

Makes 3 dozen

3 cups rolled oats	**750 ml**
1/2 cup long shred coconut	**125 ml**
1/2 cup VE Pure Cocoa	**125 ml**
2 cups white sugar	**500 ml**
1/2 cup butter	**125 ml**
1/2 cup milk	**125 ml**
1 tsp VE Vanilla Extract	**5 ml**

1. Mix together, oats, coconut and VE Pure Cocoa in mixing bowl.
2. Combine sugar, butter and milk in medium saucepan, over medium high heat. Boil for 5 minutes without stirring.
3. Remove from heat, add VE Vanilla Extract and rolled oat mixture. Stir quickly.
4. Drop by teaspoonful onto parchment lined bun pan. Cool and store in airtight tin.

VE Pure Cocoa
VE Vanilla Extract

10. Chocolate Chip Nut Cookies

Makes 3 dozen

1/2 cup vegetable oil	**125 ml**
1/2 cup soft butter	**125 ml**
1 cup packed brown sugar	**250 ml**
1/2 cup white sugar	**125 ml**
2 eggs	**2**
2 tsp VE Vanilla Extract	**10 ml**
2 cups all-purpose flour	**500 ml**
1 tsp baking soda	**5 ml**
1 tsp salt	**5 ml**
1 cup chopped nuts	**250 ml**
1 cup VE Belgian Chocolate (Dark, Milk or White)	**250 ml**

1. Preheat oven to 350°F (175°C).
2. Cream butter, oil and both sugars until smooth.
3. Add eggs one at a time. Beat in VE Vanilla Extract.
4. Add flour, baking soda and salt. Beat to a smooth dough.
5. Fold in chocolate and nuts. Drop by teaspoon onto parchment lined bun pans. Bake 10 to 12 minutes.

VE Vanilla Extract
VE Belgian Chocolate (Dark, Milk or White)

11. Cocoa and Hazelnut Meringue Puffs

Makes 3 dozen

2 egg whites	**2**
1/2 cup white sugar	**125 ml**
1/2 tsp salt	**2.5 ml**
1 tsp VE Vanilla Extract	**5 ml**
1/2 tsp white vinegar	**2.5 ml**
4 tsp VE Pure Cocoa	**20 ml**
1 cup finely chopped hazelnuts	**250 ml**

1. Preheat oven to 300°F (150°C).
2. Beat egg whites until soft peaks form. Gradually add sugar and salt. Continue beating until meringue becomes quite stiff and sugar has been completely dissolved. Beat in VE Vanilla Extract and white vinegar.
3. Combine hazelnuts and VE Pure Cocoa. Fold into meringue mixture.
4. Drop by teaspoon onto parchment lined bun pan. Bake for 30 minutes. Turn off heat and leave cookies in oven until cold (or overnight).

VE Vanilla Extract
VE Pure Cocoa

Cakes, Cupcakes, Brownies and Squares

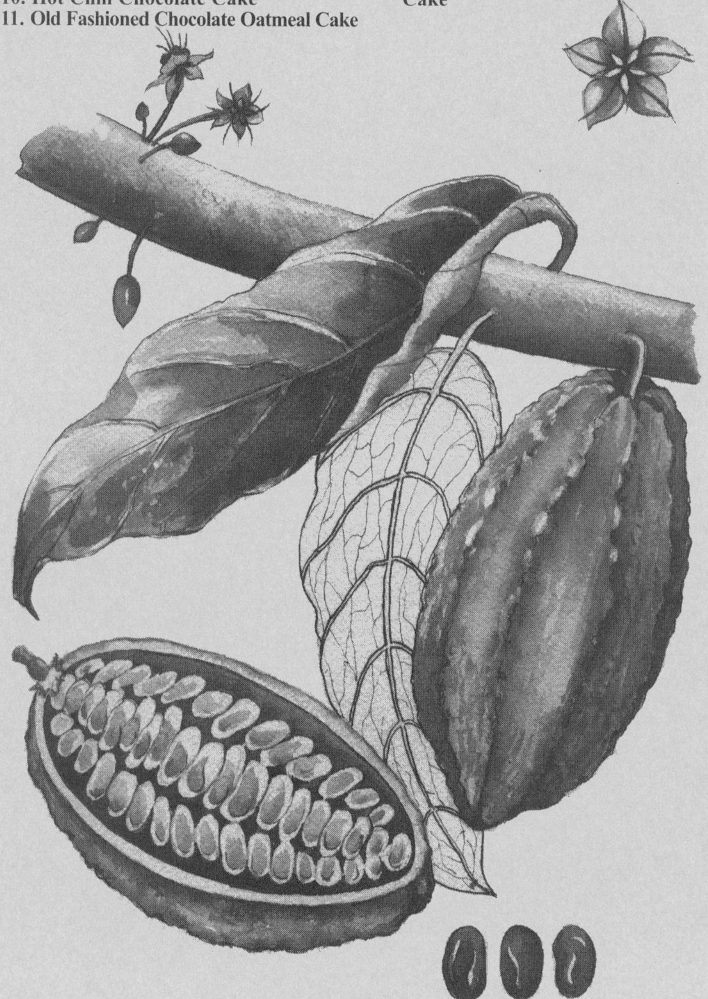

1. Low Fat Brownies - Yes Really!!

Makes 16 brownies

1/2 cup VE Pure Cocoa	**125 ml**
1 cup all-purpose flour	**250 ml**
1 tsp VE Baking Powder	**5 ml**
1/2 tsp salt	**2.5 ml**
2 Tbsp unsalted butter	**30 ml**
1 1/2 cups white sugar	**375 ml**
2 egg whites	**2**
1/2 cup unsweetened applesauce	**125 ml**
1 tsp VE Vanilla Extract	**5 ml**

1. Preheat oven to 350°F (175°C). Lightly spray an 8" (20 cm) square pan with vegetable oil.
2. Sift VE Pure Cocoa, flour, VE Baking Powder and salt into medium mixing bowl.
3. In large bowl, beat together butter and sugar. Whisk in egg whites, applesauce and VE Vanilla Extract.
4. Stir flour mixture into butter/applesauce mixture until just combined.
5. Pour into prepared pan. Bake for 35 to 40 minutes. Cool in pan. Cut into squares.
6. For a decorative touch, using a stainless steel strainer or dredger, sift icing sugar or VE Pure Cocoa over surface.

VE Pure Cocoa
VE Baking Powder
VE Vanilla Extract

2. RICH COCOA BROWNIES

Makes 24 - 36 brownies

1 cup butter	**250 ml**
1 cup white sugar	**250 ml**
1 cup packed brown sugar	**250 ml**
3/4 cup VE Pure Cocoa	**180 ml**
3 whole eggs	**3**
1 cup all-purpose flour	**250 ml**
1 1/2 tsp VE Baking Powder	**7.5 ml**
1 1/2 tsp VE Vanilla Extract	**7.5 ml**
1 cup walnut pieces	**250 ml**

1. Preheat oven to 350°F (175°C).
2. Lightly spray a 9 x 13" (23 x 33 cm) pan with vegetable oil.
3. Melt butter in large bowl. Add both sugars and VE Pure Cocoa and stir well.
4. Add eggs, one at a time, beating well after each addition. Add VE Vanilla Extract.
5. Whisk together flour and VE Baking Powder. Combine both mixtures, add walnuts and pour into prepared pan.
6. Bake 25 to 30 minutes. Cool on wire rack.
7. Dust with VE Pure Cocoa or icing sugar.

VE Pure Cocoa
VE Baking Powder
Vanilla Extract

CHOCOLATE DECADENCE MADE EASY

For a quick, decadent dessert, cut each brownie into 2 triangles. Place the brownie halves standing up in the middle of a dessert plate. Arrange **VE Brandied Cherries** on plate. Drizzle with **VE Belgian Chocolate Sauce** (see page 64)
Using a dredger or stainless steel strainer dust finished plate with **VE Pure Cocoa**.

VE Cherries in Brandy & **VE Pure Cocoa**
VE Belgian Chocolate Sauce (page 64)

3. TURTLE BROWNIES

Makes 24 - 36 brownies

1 cup butter	**250 ml**
1/2 cup VE Belgian Dark Chocolate	**125 ml**
4 eggs, beaten	**4**
1 3/4 cups white sugar	**430 ml**
2 tsp Vanilla Extract	**10 ml**
1 1/4 cups all-purpose flour	**310 ml**
1/2 tsp salt	**2.5 ml**

Topping:

1/2 cup whipping cream	**125 ml**
1/2 cup brown sugar	**125 ml**
1/4 cup butter	**60 ml**
1 1/2 cups pecan halves	**375 ml**
1 cup VE Belgian Dark Chocolate	**250 ml**

1. Preheat oven to 400°F (205°C). Lightly butter a 9 x 13" (23 x 33 cm) pan, dust with flour, shaking out the excess.
2. In double boiler or microwave, melt butter and VE Belgian Dark Chocolate stirring well.
3. Whisk together sugar, salt and VE Vanilla Extract. Add eggs one at a time. Add butter and chocolate mixture.
4. Add flour, beat well and pour into prepared pan.
5. Bake for 12 minutes (brownie will be partially baked at this point). Remove from oven and sprinkle with pecans.
6. For the topping, boil whipping cream, butter and brown sugar for 3 minutes. Pour over brownies and return to oven for 10 minutes. Remove from oven and sprinkle with 1 cup (250 ml) VE Belgian Dark Chocolate. After 2 minutes slightly swirl the chocolate. Let Turtle Brownies cool on wire rack, then cut into squares.

VE Belgian Dark Chocolate
Vanilla Extract

4. MOCHA BROWNIES

Makes 16 brownies

1/2 cup VE Dark Chocolate	125 ml
1/4 cup butter	60 ml
1 cup brown sugar	250 ml
2 eggs	2
1 Tbsp instant coffee granules, dissolved in 1 Tbsp hot water	15 ml 15 ml
3/4 cup all-purpose flour	180 ml
1/2 tsp VE Baking Powder	2.5 ml
pinch of salt	
1/2 cup chopped walnuts	125 ml

1. Preheat oven to 350°F (175°C). Lightly spray an 8" (20 cm) pan with vegetable oil and line with parchment paper.
2. In a saucepan over low heat, melt chocolate and butter.
3. In a medium stainless steel bowl, beat sugar and eggs until light. Fold in chocolate mixture and dissolved coffee until evenly mixed.
4. Sift all dry ingredients over creamed mixture. Add nuts, fold together and pour into prepared pan. Bake 25 to 30 minutes. Cool on wire cake rack for 30 minutes. Cut into squares. Dust with VE Pure Cocoa and serve.

VE Dark Chocolate
VE Baking Powder

5. FUDGE BROWNIES

Makes 16 brownies

1 cup butter, melted	**250 ml**
1 cup white sugar	**250 ml**
1 cup brown sugar	**250 ml**
2 eggs	**2**
1 cup all-purpose flour	**250 ml**
1/2 cup VE Pure Cocoa	**125 ml**
2 tsp VE Baking Powder	**10 ml**
1 tsp VE Vanilla Extract	**5 ml**

1. Preheat oven to 350°F (175°C). Lightly butter and flour an 8" (20 cm) square pan, shaking out excess flour.
2. Sift flour, VE Pure Cocoa and VE Baking Powder together in one bowl.
3. Beat eggs, add melted butter, VE Vanilla Extract and both sugars. Combine both mixes and pour into prepared pan.
4. Bake for 30 minutes. Cool, then ice (with Quick Creamy Icing page 66 or Chocolate Fudge Icing page 61), or dust lightly with VE Pure Cocoa or icing sugar. Cut in squares.

VE Pure Cocoa
VE Baking Powder
VE Vanilla Extract

6. DOUBLE FUDGE CHOCOLATE CUPCAKES

Makes 24 cupcakes or 12 cupcakes plus 1 - 8" (20 cm) round cake

2 eggs	**2**
1 cup white sugar	**250 ml**
2 Tbsp softened butter	**30 ml**
1 cup vegetable oil	**250 ml**
1/2 cup VE Pure Cocoa	**125 ml**
1/2 cup buttermilk	**125 ml**
1 tsp VE Vanilla Extract	**5 ml**
2 1/4 cup flour	**560 ml**
1 1/2 tsp baking soda	**7.5 ml**
1 1/2 tsp VE Baking Powder	**7.5 ml**
1 cup boiling water	**250 ml**

1. Preheat oven to 350°F (175°C).
2. Lightly spray VE Classic Muffin Pan(s) with vegetable oil or line with paper cups.
3. In medium stainless steel mixing bowl, beat together first 7 ingredients in order, adding one ingredient at a time.
4. In small stainless steel mixing bowl, sift together dry ingredients.
5. Combine wet and dry ingredients. Stir in boiling water until batter is very smooth.
6. Pour into prepared pans and bake for 20 to 25 minutes. Cool on stainless steel cooling rack.
7. Ice with Chocolate Fudge Icing (see page 61)

VE Pure Cocoa
VE Vanilla Extract
VE Baking Powder

7. Double Chocolate Zucchini Cake

Makes 9 X 13" (23 x 33 cm) pan

2 1/2 cups VE Pure Cocoa	**625 ml**
1 tsp baking soda	**5 ml**
1 tsp salt	**5 ml**
1/2 cup butter	**125 ml**
1/2 cup vegetable oil	**125 ml**
1 3/4 cups sugar	**430 ml**
2 eggs	**2**
1 tsp VE Vanilla Extract	**5 ml**
1/2 cup buttermilk	**125 ml**
2 cups grated zucchini	**500 ml**
2/3 cup VE Belgian Dark Chocolate	**160 ml**
3/4 cup walnut pieces	**180 ml**

1. Preheat oven to 325°F (160°C). Lightly spray a 9 x 13" (23 x 33 cm) pan with vegetable oil.
2. Cream together butter, oil, sugar, eggs, VE Vanilla Extract and buttermilk.
3. Sift together dry ingredients and add to creamed mixture.
4. Fold in zucchini and pour into prepared pan. Sprinkle with walnut pieces and VE Belgian Dark Chocolate.
5. Bake for 45 minutes.

VE Pure Cocoa
VE Vanilla Extract
VE Belgian Dark Chocolate

8. INDIVIDUAL BROWNIE CHEESECAKE

Makes 12 cupcakes

1/2 cup butter, softened	**125 ml**
1 cup white sugar	**250 ml**
2 eggs	**2**
1 tsp VE Vanilla Extract	**5 ml**
1/2 cup sifted VE Pure Cocoa	**125 ml**
1/2 cup all-purpose flour	**125 ml**
1/4 tsp salt	**1.25 ml**
1 egg yolk	**1**
1 - 4 oz brick-style cream cheese	**125 ml**

1. Lightly spray Classic Muffin Pan with vegetable oil or line with paper cups.
2. Preheat oven to 325°F (160°C).
3. In large bowl, beat butter with 3/4 cup (180 ml) of white sugar. Beat until light and fluffy.
4. Add whole eggs, one at a time, beating well after each addition. Add VE Vanilla Extract.
5. Sift together flour, VE Pure Cocoa and salt. Add to creamed mixture, stirring well to combine.
6. Spoon into muffin cups.
7. Cream together remaining sugar, egg yolk and cream cheese. Spoon over chocolate mixture and swirl slightly with a fork.
8. Bake for 30 minutes. Let cool in pan on cooling rack. Lightly dust with icing sugar before serving.

VE Vanilla Extract
VE Pure Cocoa

9. BLACK MAGIC CHOCOLATE CAKE

Makes a 9 x 13" (23 x 33 cm) cake

1 3/4 cups all-purpose flour	**430 ml**
2 cups white sugar	**500 ml**
3/4 cup VE Pure Cocoa	**180 ml**
2 tsp baking soda	**10 ml**
1 tsp VE Baking Powder	**5 ml**
1 tsp salt	**5 ml**
2 eggs	**2**
1/2 cup vegetable oil	**125 ml**
1 cup cold, strong coffee	**250 ml**
1 cup buttermilk	**250 ml**
1 tsp VE Vanilla Extract (or VE Peppermint for a Chocolate Mint Cake)	**5 ml**

1. Preheat oven to 350°F (175°C). Lightly spray a 9 x 13" (23 x 33 cm) baking pan with vegetable oil.
2. Whisk together flour, sugar, VE Pure Cocoa, baking soda, VE Baking Powder and salt into mixing bowl.
3. Add eggs, oil, coffee, buttermilk and VE Vanilla Extract. Beat with an electric mixer at medium speed for 2 minutes. Pour batter into prepared pan.
4. Bake for 40 minutes or until toothpick inserted in centre of cake comes out clean.
5. Dust with icing sugar, VE Pure Cocoa or ice with our recipe for Quick Creamy Icing (page 66) or Chocolate Fudge Icing (page 61).

VE Pure Cocoa
VE Baking Powder
VE Vanilla Extract or VE Peppermint

10. HOT CHILI CHOCOLATE CAKE

For a really innovative cake, add 1 tsp (5 ml) finely ground **VE Chili Flakes** to the Black Magic Chocolate Cake batter. Dust the finished cake with **VE Pure Cocoa** and for an extra touch, decorate with a couple of fresh chilies to let people know they are in for a special treat. The richness of the chocolate chili combination would be an ideal finish to a Mexican feast.

11. Old Fashioned Chocolate Oatmeal Cake

Makes a 9 x 13" (23 x 33 cm) pan

1 cup oat flakes	**250 ml**
2 cups boiling water	**500 ml**
1/2 cup VE Pure Cocoa	**125 ml**
4 eggs	**4**
1 cup butter	**250 ml**
3 cups loosely packed brown sugar	**750 ml**
2 cups all-purpose flour	**500 ml**
2 tsp VE Vanilla Extract	**10 ml**
2 tsp VE Baking Powder	**10 ml**
2 tsp baking soda	**10 ml**

1. Preheat oven to 375°F (190°C). Lightly spray a 9 x 13" (23 x 33 cm) pan with vegetable oil.
2. Pour boiling water over oat flakes and let cool to room temperature.
3. Combine VE Pure Cocoa and brown sugar, mixing until lump free. Add butter and cream well.
4. Add eggs, one at a time, beating well after each addition. Add VE Vanilla Extract.
5. Whisk together flour, VE Baking Powder and baking soda. Add to creamed mixture, stir well.
6. Add cooled oatmeal, pour into prepared pan and bake for 35 to 40 minutes.

Note: This cake is incredibly moist, and keeps well for several days.

VE Pure Cocoa
VE Vanilla Extract
VE Baking Powder

12. CHOCOLATE VELVET CHEESECAKE

Makes 1 - 9 1/2" (24 cm)

Crust:

2 cups chocolate wafer crumbs	**250 ml**
1/4 cup melted butter	**60 ml**

Filling:

1 1/2 lb brick-style cream cheese	**750 g**
1 cup white sugar	**250 ml**
5 whole eggs	**5**
1 Tbsp VE Vanilla Extract	**15 ml**
3/4 cup sour cream	**180 ml**
1/4 lb melted VE Belgian Dark Chocolate	**125 g**

1. Preheat oven at 350ºF (175ºC). Mix together crust ingredients and press into bottom of 9 1/2" (24 cm) Spring Form Pan. Bake in oven for 5 minutes. Lower heat to 325ºF (160ºC).
2. Beat cream cheese with sugar until smooth. Add VE Vanilla Extract. Add eggs, one at a time, beating well after each addition. Add sour cream and beat to form a smooth batter. Add melted chocolate.
3. Pour over baked crust. Bake at 325ºF (160ºC) for 40 minutes. **Tip**: Place a pan of cold water in the bottom of the oven while the cheesecake bakes. This will help promote even baking and prevent the cake from cracking.
4. Remove the cheesecake from the oven, let cool to room temperature. Refrigerate overnight in the pan.
5. To serve, remove the outside ring and place the Chocolate Velvet Cheesecake on a plate. For best results when serving cheesecake, always use a clean, wet knife for each slice. Serve with Raspberry Coulis (page 46).

For a really great decorative touch, melt some VE Belgian Chocolate Sauce (see page 64) over hot water, and with a spoon drizzle the sauce over the surface. Chill until the sauce sets then serve. A chocolate lover's dream!

VE Belgian Dark Chocolate
VE Vanilla Extract

13. BANANA COCOA COFFEE CAKE

Makes 1 cake

1 1/2 cups mashed ripe bananas	**375 ml**
1 cup sour cream	**250 ml**
1 1/4 cup all-purpose flour	**310 ml**
3/4 cup VE Pure Cocoa	**180 ml**
1 1/2 tsp baking soda	**7.5 ml**
1/2 tsp VE Nutmeg	**2.5 ml**
3/4 tsp salt	**3.75 ml**
3/4 cup butter, at room temperature	**180 ml**
1 1/2 cups sugar	**375 ml**
3 large eggs	**3**
1 Bundt pan	**1**

1. Preheat oven to 350°F (175°C). Butter and flour Bundt pan, shake out excess flour.
2. In a mixing bowl, mix together bananas and sour cream. Set aside.
3. Sift together flour, VE Pure Cocoa, baking soda, VE Nutmeg and salt.
4. Cream butter and sugar until fluffy. Add eggs, one at a time, beating well after each addition.
5. Add half of banana mixture, beating well. Add half of dry ingredients and beat well. Repeat.
6. Pour into prepared pan. Bake 55 to 60 minutes or until a toothpick inserted in centre comes out clean.

VE Pure Cocoa
VE Nutmeg

14. FAT-FREE CHOCOLATE CAKE

Makes 1 - 9” (23 cm) cake

1 1/4 cups all-purpose flour	**310 ml**
1 cup white sugar	**250 ml**
1/2 cup VE Pure Cocoa	**125 ml**
1/4 cup cornstarch	**60 ml**
1/2 tsp baking soda	**2.5 ml**
1/2 tsp salt	**2.5 ml**
4 egg whites	**4**
1 cup water	**250 ml**
1 tsp VE Vanilla Extract	**5 ml**
1/2 cup dark corn syrup	**125 ml**

1. Preheat oven to 350°F (175°C).
2. Whisk together first 6 ingredients in medium bowl.
3. In second bowl, whisk together egg whites, water, VE Vanilla Extract and corn syrup. Pour into centre of dry ingredients stirring until smooth.
4. Pour into lightly sprayed 9" (23 cm) square pan. Bake for 30 minutes or until a toothpick inserted in centre comes out clean.
5. Dust with icing sugar or VE Pure Cocoa and serve.

VE Pure Cocoa
VE Vanilla Extract

15. CHOCOLATE CRANBERRY LOAF

Makes 1 loaf

1/2 cup butter	125 ml
1 cup white sugar	250 ml
2 large eggs	2
1 tsp VE Vanilla Extract	5 ml
1 1/4 cups frozen cranberries, chopped	310 ml
3/4 cup milk	180 ml
2 cups all-purpose flour	500 ml
1/3 cup VE Pure Cocoa	80 ml
1 tsp VE Baking Powder	5 ml
1 tsp baking soda	5 ml
1/4 tsp salt	1.25 ml
1/2 cup VE Belgian Dark or Milk Chocolate	125 ml
1/2 cup chopped walnuts	125 ml

1. Preheat oven to 350°F (175ºC). Lightly butter a 9 x 5 x 3" (23 x 13 x 8 cm) loaf pan and dust with flour.
2. Cream butter and sugar in large bowl. Beat in eggs one at a time. Add VE Vanilla Extract, cranberries and milk.
3. Place remaining ingredients in 2nd bowl. Pour batter into centre. Combine in swift strokes to just moisten the mixture. Turn into prepared loaf pan. Bake 1 hour or until a toothpick inserted in centre comes out clean.
4. Remove from oven and let stand for 10 minutes before turning out onto a cooling rack.

VE Vanilla Extract
VE Pure Cocoa
VE Baking Powder
VE Belgian Dark or Milk Chocolate

16. Nanaimo Bars

Makes a 9 x 13" (23 x 33 cm) pan

Base:

1/2 cup butter	**125 ml**
1/4 cup brown sugar	**60 ml**
1 egg	**1**
1 tsp VE Vanilla Extract	**5 ml**
2 cups graham wafer crumbs	**500 ml**
1/2 cup walnut crumbs	**125 ml**
1 cup coconut	**250 ml**
1/4 cup VE Pure Cocoa	**60 ml**

Middle Layer:

1/4 cup butter	**60 ml**
1 Tbsp milk	**15 ml**
2 Tbsp custard powder	**30 ml**
2 cups icing sugar	**500 ml**

Topping:

1/2 cup VE Dark Belgian Chocolate	**125 ml**
1 Tbsp butter	**15 ml**

1. For the base, combine butter, sugar, VE Pure Cocoa, VE Vanilla Extract and egg in double boiler over simmering water. Stir until mixture resembles custard. Add coconut, graham wafer crumbs and walnut crumbs. Press into 9 x 13" (23 x 33 cm) pan to form base.
2. For the middle layer, cream butter with icing sugar, custard powder and thin with milk. Spread over base and let sit for 15 minutes.
3. Melt chocolate with butter until smooth, pour over top. Let set and cut in squares with a hot, dry knife.

VE Vanilla Extract
VE Pure Cocoa
VE Dark Belgian Chocolate

17. BLACK FOREST SHORTCAKES

Serves 6

Shortcakes

2 1/4 cups all-purpose flour	**560 ml**
1/2 cup white sugar	**125 ml**
1/3 cup VE Pure Cocoa	**80 ml**
1 Tbsp VE Baking Powder	**15 ml**
1/2 tsp baking soda	**2.5 ml**
1/2 tsp salt	**2.5 ml**
1/2 cup cold butter, cubed	**125 ml**
1/2 cup sour cream	**125 ml**
1/2 cup milk	**125 ml**

1. Preheat oven to 425°F (220°C).
2. In a bowl sift flour, sugar, VE Pure Cocoa, VE Baking Powder, baking soda and salt. Using a pastry blender, cut in cubed butter.
3. Whisk together sour cream and milk. Add to dry ingredients, stirring to make a soft, slightly sticky dough.
4. Turn out onto a lightly floured board and knead 8 times until smooth. Pat out to an 8" (20 cm) circle. Using a 3" (8 cm) cutter, cut out 6 rounds. Place on a parchment lined bun pan. Bake for 15 minutes. Transfer to a rack and cool.

Continued on next page

VE Pure Cocoa
VE Baking Powder

BLACK FOREST SHORTCAKES (CONTINUED)

Cherry Sauce:

1 jar VE Cherries in Brandy	**1**
1 Tbsp cornstarch	**15 ml**
1/2 tsp VE Almond Extract	**2.5 ml**

1. Strain cherries from juice. Remove pits from cherries and set cherries aside.
2. Slowly add 1/4 cup (60 ml) cherry juice to cornstarch to create thin paste.
3. Heat remaining juice to boiling, slowly add some of the hot juice to the cornstarch mixture, stirring continuously. Add this to the hot juice, return to boil stirring until thickened. Remove from heat. Stir in cherries, VE Almond Extract and cool.

Whipped Cream:

1/2 cup whipping cream	**125 ml**
1 tsp VE Vanilla Extract	**5 ml**
2 tsp icing sugar	**10 ml**

1. Combine and whip to soft peaks.

Assemble:

1. Slice shortcakes in half. Place bottom halves on dessert plates.
2. Divide cherry sauce between 6 shortcakes. Top with whipped cream.
3. Replace top halves. Dust with icing sugar or VE Pure Cocoa.

VE Cherries in Brandy
VE Almond Extract
VE Vanilla Extract

18. White Chocolate and Raspberry Cheesecake

Serves 8 to 10

Crust:

2 cups graham wafer crumbs	**500 ml**
1/4 cup melted butter	**60 ml**

Filling:

1 1/2 lbs cream cheese	**750 g**
1 cup white sugar	**250 ml**
5 whole eggs	**5**
2 tsp VE Vanilla Extract	**10 ml**
3/4 cup sour cream	**180 ml**
1 cup melted VE Belgian White Chocolate	**250 ml**
1 cup fresh or frozen raspberries	**250 ml**

1. Combine graham wafer crumbs and butter. Press into 9" (23 cm) spring form pan. Bake at 350°F (175°C) for 5 minutes.
2. Beat cream cheese and sugar until smooth. Add eggs one at a time, beating well after each addition. Add VE Vanilla Extract and melted VE Belgian White Chocolate.
3. Pour half of the batter into pan. Sprinkle with raspberries and pour remaining batter over top. Bake at 325°F (160°C) for 40 minutes.
   Tip:Place a pan of cold water in the bottom of the oven while the cheesecake bakes. This will promote even baking and prevent the cheesecake from cracking.
4. Remove the cheesecake from the oven, let cool to room temperature. Refrigerate overnight in the pan. To serve, gently remove outer ring and transfer to a serving plate. Serve with Raspberry Coulis.

VE Vanilla Extract & VE Belgian White Chocolate

Raspberry Coulis

1-12 oz (340 ml) package of frozen raspberries in light syrup, thawed and blended. If you wish to have a seedless sauce, press gently through a strainer.

19. DARK OR WHITE FLOURLESS CHOCOLATE CAKE

Serves 8 to 10

1 1/4 cup butter	**310 ml**
1 lb VE Dark or White Belgian Chocolate	**454 g**
10 eggs, separated	**10**
1 1/2 cups white sugar	**375 ml**

1. Preheat oven to 250°F (120°C). Lightly butter spring form pan and dust with flour shaking out excess.
2. Melt butter and chocolate in a stainless steel bowl over simmering (not boiling) water. Stir frequently.
3. While the chocolate is melting, beat egg yolks and 1 1/4 cups (310 ml) sugar until very thick (about 10 minutes).
4. With a spatula, fold melted chocolate into beaten egg yolks.
5. Whip egg whites with remaining sugar until very stiff.
6. Fold meringue into chocolate mixture. Fill spring form pan and bake for 2 hours. Insert a toothpick into the centre of the cake. If it comes out dry, the cake is done.
7. Remove cake from oven and place on a rack to cool. Open the pan carefully and remove the cake to a serving plate. Serve warm or at room temperature, dust with VE Pure Cocoa or icing sugar.

VE Dark or **White Belgian Chocolate**

Chocolate Desserts including Pudding, Mousse, Pies and Chocolate Fondue

1. Hot Fudge Pudding
2. Chocolate Pecan Pie
3. White Chocolate Mousse (and White Chocolate Mousse Pie)
4. Chilled Chocolate Cream Pie
5. Chocolate Pudding
6. Classic Chocolate Mousse
7. Chocolate Fondue

1. HOT FUDGE PUDDING

Serves 6 to 8

1 cup all-purpose flour	250 ml
2/3 cup white sugar	160 ml
1/4 cup VE Pure Cocoa	60 ml
2 tsp VE Baking Powder	10 ml
1/4 tsp salt	1.25 ml
1/2 cup milk	125 ml
2 Tbsp melted butter	30 ml
1 cup walnut pieces (optional)	250 ml

Topping:

1 cup brown sugar	250 ml
1/4 cup VE Pure Cocoa	60 ml
1 3/4 cups boiling water	430 ml

1. Preheat oven to 350°F (175°C). Lightly spray an 8" (20 cm) square pan with vegetable oil.
2. Sift together flour, sugar, VE Baking Powder, VE Pure Cocoa and salt.
3. Pour in milk, melted butter and walnut pieces and stir. Batter will be very thick.
4. Spread batter in bottom of pan. Whisk topping ingredients and pour over batter. DO NOT STIR.
5. Bake for 30 minutes. There will be a rich chocolate sauce on the bottom of the pan.
6. Serve warm with ice cream or whipped cream.

VE Pure Cocoa
VE Baking Powder

2. Chocolate Pecan Pie

Makes 9" (23 cm) Flan Pan

Crust:

1 2/3 cup all-purpose flour	**410 ml**
1/4 cup white sugar	**60 ml**
1/2 tsp salt	**2.5 ml**
6 Tbsp cold butter	**90 ml**
2 egg yolks	**2**
1 tsp VE Vanilla Extract	**5 ml**
1 Tbsp cold water	**15 ml**
Filling on next page	

1. Whisk together flour, sugar and salt.
2. Using a pastry blender, cut in butter until mixture resembles coarse crumbs.
3. Whisk together egg yolks, water and VE Vanilla Extract. Pour into flour mixture. Using a wooden spoon, stir until a ball begins to form.
4. Turn out into a 9" (23 cm) flan pan and press dough to form shell (no need to roll). Start by forming the sides first and then flatten out the bottom.
5. Place in refrigerator for 30 minutes.

Continued on next page

CHOCOLATE PECAN PIE (CONTINUED)

Filling:

4 eggs	**4**
1 cup dark brown sugar	**250 ml**
3/4 cup corn syrup	**180 ml**
1/2 tsp salt	**1.25 ml**
1/4 cup melted butter	**60 ml**
1 tsp VE Vanilla Extract	**5 ml**
2 cups pecan halves	**500 ml**
1 Tbsp all-purpose flour	**15 ml**

1. Preheat oven to 400°F (205°C).
2. Cover bottom of refrigerated pie crust (see previous page) with pecan halves. Place flan pan on parchment lined bun pan.
3. Whisk eggs in stainless steel bowl. Add brown sugar, corn syrup and salt, beating well.
4. Whisk in melted butter, VE Vanilla Extract and flour.
5. Pour over pecans. Bake in centre of oven for 10 minutes.
6. Reduce temperature to 325°F (160°C) and bake for 30 minutes, or until set.
7. Remove from oven and let cool on cake rack. Remove outer ring from flan pan and transfer pie to serving plate.

Topping:

1/2 cup VE Dark Belgian Chocolate	**125 ml**
1 Tbsp butter	**15 ml**
1/2 cup whipping cream	**125 ml**

1. Bring cream to a boil. Remove from heat. Add chocolate and butter, stirring until melted. Drizzle over cooled pecan pie.

VE Vanilla Extract
VE Dark Belgian Chocolate

3. WHITE CHOCOLATE MOUSSE

Serves 4

1 tsp gelatin	**5 ml**
1/4 cup cold water	**60 ml**
3/4 cup VE Belgian White Chocolate	**180 ml**
1/3 cup milk	**80 ml**
1 1/2 cups whipping cream	**375 ml**
1 tsp VE Vanilla Extract	**5 ml**

1. Dissolve gelatin in cold water.
2. Scald milk, remove from heat, add VE Belgian White Chocolate, stirring until melted.
3. Gently heat gelatine until melted. Add to melted chocolate, stir and refrigerate for 10 minutes.
4. Whip cream with VE Vanilla Extract.
5. Fold melted chocolate mixture into whipped cream. Pour into dessert glasses and refrigerate until set, at least 1 hour.

Variations

1. Fold in fresh raspberries, blackberries or blueberries and then spoon into dessert glasses.
2. Place fresh fruit in bottom of glass, drizzle with liqueur and then top with mousse.
3. Decorate mousse by placing an edible flower on top.
4. **WHITE CHOCOLATE MOUSSE PIE:** White chocolate mousse may be poured into a chocolate wafer crumb pie shell and chilled or frozen for a make ahead dessert. Dust with **VE Pure Cocoa**, or drizzle with melted dark or milk chocolate before serving.

VE Belgian White Chocolate
VE Vanilla Extract

4. Chilled Chocolate Cream Pie

9" (23 cm) pie - Serves 6 to 8

Crust:

1 1/2 cups chocolate wafer crumbs	**375 ml**
3 Tbsp granulated sugar	**45 ml**
1/3 cup melted butter	**80 ml**

1. Combine ingredients and press into 9" (23 cm) pie plate. Bake at 325°F (160°C) for 12 minutes. Cool on wire rack.

Filling:

1/3 cup VE Belgian Dark or Milk Chocolate, melted	**80 ml**
3/4 cup room temperature butter	**180 ml**
1 cup white sugar	**250 ml**
2 tsp VE Vanilla Extract	**10 ml**
3 large eggs	**3**
1 cup whipped cream	**250 ml**

1. Cream butter and sugar with electric mixer until light and fluffy.
2. Beat in VE Vanilla Extract and melted chocolate.
3. Add eggs one at a time, beating 5 minutes after each addition. Pour the filling into chilled shell and return to the refrigerator until set.
4. Before serving, top the pie with whipped cream and dust with VE Pure Cocoa.

VE Belgian Dark or **Milk Chocolate**
VE Vanilla Extract

5. CHOCOLATE PUDDING

Serves 4

1/2 cup white sugar	**125 ml**
1/3 cup VE Pure Cocoa	**80 ml**
3 Tbsp cornstarch	**45 ml**
pinch of salt	**pinch**
1/3 cup water	**80 ml**
2 cups whole milk	**500 ml**
1 tsp VE Vanilla Extract	**5 ml**
1 Tbsp butter	**15 ml**

1. Whisk together, white sugar, cornstarch, salt and VE Pure Cocoa.
2. Stir in water to make a thin paste.
3. Heat milk to scalding. Add a ladle of hot milk to chocolate mixture, stirring well.
4. Add chocolate mix in steady stream to hot milk, bring to a boil, stirring constantly. Remove from heat, whisk in VE Vanilla Extract and butter. Pour into serving dishes, cover and let cool before serving.

VE Pure Cocoa
VE Vanilla Extract

6. CLASSIC CHOCOLATE MOUSSE

Serves 4

1/2 cup VE Belgian Dark Chocolate, melted	**125 ml**
3 eggs, separated	**3**
1 Tbsp white sugar	**15 ml**
3 Tbsp strong coffee	**45 ml**
1 Tbsp brandy or orange liqueur	**15 ml**
1 cup whipping cream, whipped to soft peaks	**250 ml**

1. Melt chocolate over hot, not boiling water.
2. Whisk egg yolks, coffee and liqueur in separate bowl.
3. Whip egg whites and sugar until soft peaks form.
4. Whisk together melted chocolate with the egg yolk mixture. Quickly fold in whipped cream.
5. With a spatula fold in the meringue. Pour into individual serving glasses or in a large dessert bowl. Chill 3 hours before serving.

Tip: For a decorative touch, drizzle the inside of glasses (or bowl) with melted dark chocolate before adding the mousse.

VE Belgian Dark Chocolate

7. CHOCOLATE FONDUE

Serves 4 to 6

1 cup heavy or whipping cream	**250 ml**
1 cup VE Belgian Dark or Milk Chocolate	**250 ml**
2 Tbsp liqueur (kirsch, brandy, orange)	**30 ml**

1. Bring light cream to a boil in a saucepan. Remove from heat.
2. Add VE Belgian Chocolate and stir until melted. Add liqueur, pour into a fondue pot and keep warm.

Dippers

apple wedges
orange segments
pineapple chunks
papaya
fresh strawberries
kiwi fruit
cubes of toasted pound cake

Note: To toast pound cake, cut in 1" (2.5 cm) cubes and bake at 375°F (190°C) until golden. Toasting the cubes will prevent crumbs in the fondue.

VE Belgian Dark or **Milk Chocolate**

Icing, Toppings & Sauces

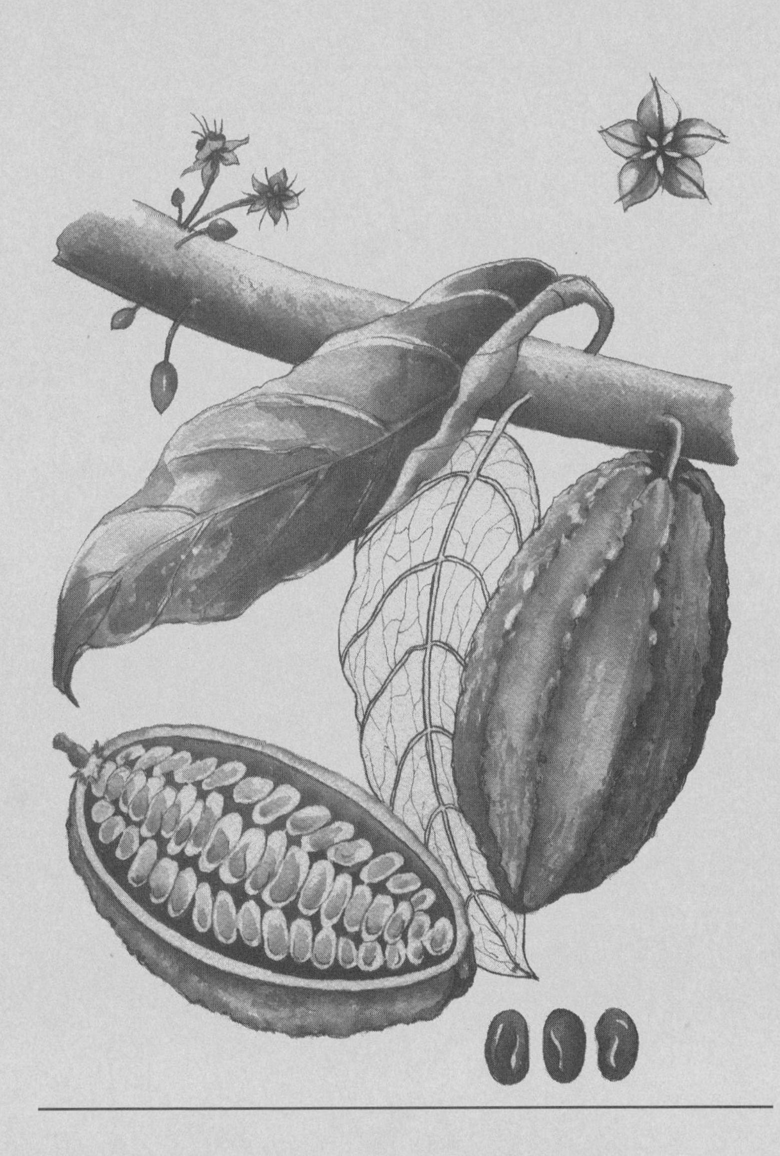

1. CHOCOLATE CREAM CHEESE ICING

Makes 2 cups (500 ml)

1/4 cup room temperature cream cheese	**60 ml**
1/4 cup VE Belgian Dark Chocolate, melted	**60 ml**
1/4 cup milk	**60 ml**
1 tsp VE Vanilla Extract	**5 ml**
4 cups icing sugar	**1 L**
pinch salt	**pinch**

1. Beat cream cheese, VE Vanilla Extract with 1 cup (250 ml) icing sugar and salt.
2. Beat in melted chocolate. Add remaining icing sugar, thinning out with milk. Beat until smooth and ready to spread.

VE Belgian Dark Chocolate, melted
VE Vanilla Extract

2. CHOCOLATE FUDGE ICING

1/2 cup soft butter	**125 ml**
1 cup sifted icing sugar	**250 ml**
2/3 cup VE Pure Cocoa	**160 ml**
1 tsp VE Vanilla Extract	**5 ml**
2 Tbsp milk	**30 ml**
2 Tbsp hot coffee	**30 ml**

1. Place butter, VE Pure Cocoa and icing sugar in food processor. Blend for 4 seconds.
2. Add VE Vanilla Extract, milk and hot coffee. Blend until very smooth. Additional milk will make a thinner icing.

VE Pure Cocoa
VE Vanilla Extract

3. CHOCOLATE GLAZE

Makes 1 cup (250 ml)

2 Tbsp VE Pure Cocoa	**30 ml**
1 Tbsp plus 2 tsp water	**25 ml**
1 Tbsp vegetable oil	**15 ml**
1 Tbsp corn syrup	**15 ml**
1 cup icing sugar	**250 ml**

1. In small saucepan over medium heat, whisk together VE Pure Cocoa, water, vegetable oil and corn syrup and cook until dissolved and smooth.
2. Remove from heat and beat in icing sugar. Immediately pour over cooled cakes, loaves or cookies and let drizzle down the sides.

VE Pure Cocoa

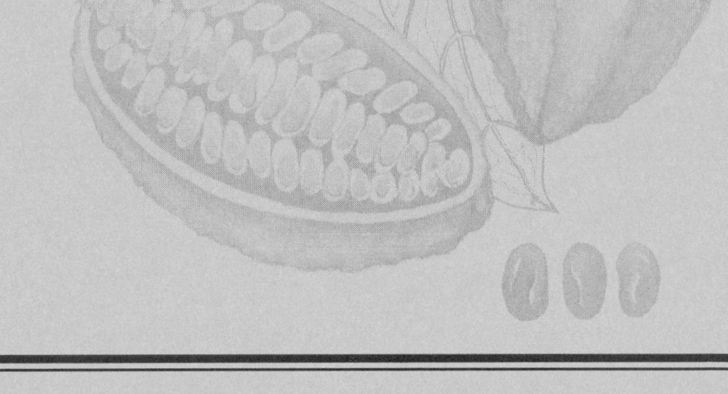

4. CHOCOLATE FUDGE SAUCE

Makes 2 1/2 cups (625 ml)

3/4 cup VE Belgian Dark Chocolate	**180 ml**
3 Tbsp butter	**45 ml**
2/3 cup water	**160 ml**
1 2/3 cups white sugar	**410 ml**
6 Tbsp corn syrup	**90 ml**
1 Tbsp VE Vanilla Extract	**15 ml**

1. Slowly melt butter and VE Belgian Dark Chocolate in heavy bottomed saucepan.
2. When chocolate and butter have melted add water and whisk together.
3. Add sugar and corn syrup and mix until smooth. Increase heat and simmer sauce without stirring for 9 minutes.
4. Remove sauce from heat, let cool for 15 minutes. Stir in VE Vanilla Extract. Serve warm sauce with ice cream, cream puffs or on angel food cake.

VE Belgian Dark Chocolate
VE Vanilla Extract

5. VE Belgian Chocolate Sauce

Makes 2 cups (500 ml)

1 cup VE Belgian Dark Chocolate	**250 g**
1/3 cup white sugar	**80 ml**
2/3 cup whipping cream	**160 ml**
2 Tbsp unsalted butter	**30 ml**

1. Combine whipping cream, butter and sugar in saucepan. Bring to a boil.
2. Remove from heat and add VE Belgian Dark Chocolate, stirring until smooth and glossy.
3. Store unused portion in refrigerator and use within 1 week.

Tips:
- May be used as a chocolate fondue, for dipping fruit on skewers, pieces of pound cake or toasted angel food cake cubes.
- Heated up as a sauce over angel food cake, brownies, ice cream or to decorate dessert plates.
- In its firm state may be used to ice cakes, brownies or cupcakes.

VE Belgian Dark Chocolate

6. CHOCOLATE SYRUP

Makes 2 cups (500 ml)

1 1/4 cups water	**310 ml**
1 1/4 cups white sugar	**310 ml**
3/4 cup VE Pure Cocoa	**180 ml**

1. In a small saucepan, dissolve sugar in water. Bring to a boil for 3 minutes.
2. Reduce heat to medium. Whisk in VE Pure Cocoa until smooth. Cool. Store covered in refrigerator.
3. To Serve: Whisk 3 Tbsp (45 ml) of Chocolate Syrup into 1 glass of milk.
4. This syrup may also be used to drizzle on ice cream and desserts.

VE Pure Cocoa

7. WHITE CHOCOLATE SAUCE

1 1/2 cups whipping cream	**375 ml**
1 cup VE Belgian White Chocolate	**250 ml**
1 tsp VE Vanilla Extract	**5 ml**

1. Heat 3/4 cup (180 ml) of whipping cream over medium high heat until cream begins to steam.
2. Place VE Belgian White Chocolate in heat proof bowl. Pour steaming cream over chocolate and stir until smooth.
3. In separate bowl, whip remaining cream. Fold one third of whipped cream into melted chocolate. Fold in remaining whipped cream and VE Vanilla Extract. Store in air tight container for up to 24 hours.
4. Try this white chocolate sauce as a drizzle over fresh fruit.

VE Belgian White Chocolate
VE Vanilla Extract

8. QUICK CREAMY ICING

Makes 1.5 cups (375 ml)

2 Tbsp softened butter	**30 ml**
2 cups icing sugar	**500 ml**
1 egg	**1**
1 to 2 Tbsp light cream	**15 to 30 ml**
1 tsp VE Vanilla Extract (VE Almond or Peppermint Extract)	**5 ml**

1. Cream butter, stir in icing sugar. Beat in egg, and add enough cream to make a spreadable consistency.
2. Flavour as desired.
3. Makes enough icing for one 8 or 9" (20 or 23 cm) square.

VE Vanilla Extract
VE Almond Extract
or **VE Peppermint Extract**

Variation: For Chocolate Icing, sift 3 Tbsp (45 ml) **VE Pure Cocoa** with the icing sugar.

Candies

1. Almond Crunch with Dark Chocolate
2. White Chocolate Bark with Dried Fruit & Nuts
3. White Chocolate Peppermint Bark
4. Five Minute Fudge
5. Cocoa Fudge
6. Chocolate Hazelnut Clusters

1. Almond Crunch with Dark Chocolate

1 Tbsp corn syrup	**15 ml**
1 1/4 cups white sugar	**310 ml**
1 cup butter	**250 ml**
1/4 cup water	**60 ml**
1 1/4 cups toasted slivered almonds	**310 ml**
3/4 cup VE Belgian Chocolate (Milk or Dark)	**180 ml**

1. In a large heavy saucepan combine syrup, sugar, butter and water. Bring to a boil for 20 minutes or until the temperature on candy thermometer reaches 300°F (150°C). Do not stir while the sugar is cooking.
2. When the temperature is reached, remove from heat and stir in toasted almonds. Pour onto a parchment lined bun pan.
3. Sprinkle pieces of VE Belgian Chocolate over surface and as they begin to melt spread with a small knife.
4. Allow to cool completely, then break into pieces.

VE Belgian Chocolate (Milk or Dark)

2. White Chocolate Bark with Dried Fruit & Nuts

1 lb VE Belgian White Chocolate	**500 g**
1 cup dried fruit (cherries, cranberries, diced dried apricots, dried blueberries or raisins)	**250 ml**
1 cup toasted almonds or pistachios	**250 ml**

1. Melt half of VE Belgian White Chocolate in top of double boiler. Remove from heat then add remaining chips and stir continuously until all chips are melted. This process will keep your chocolate very liquid and shiny.
2. Add dried fruit and nuts and using a spatula, quickly scrape onto a parchment lined bun pan. Refrigerate for at least 1 hour, then break up into bite sized pieces.

VE Belgian White Chocolate

3. White Chocolate Peppermint Bark

1 lb VE Belgian White Chocolate	**500 g**
1 cup coarsely crushed candy canes	**250 ml**

1. Melt VE Belgian White Chocolate over hot water, stirring frequently.
2. Quickly stir in crushed peppermint candy and using a spatula, scrape out onto a parchment lined bun pan. Let set in refrigerator for 1 hour. Break into pieces and watch it disappear!

VE Belgian White Chocolate

4. Five Minute Fudge

2/3 cup evaporated milk	**160 ml**
1 1/2 cups white sugar	**375 ml**
1/2 tsp salt	**2.5 ml**
1 1/4 cups VE Dark or Milk Chocolate	**310 ml**
16 regular sized marshmallows	**16**
1 tsp VE Vanilla Extract	**5 ml**
1/2 cup chopped nuts (walnuts or pecans)	**125 ml**

1. Combine in saucepan evaporated milk, sugar and salt. Bring to a boil. Cook for 5 minutes stirring frequently.
2. Remove from heat, stir in remaining ingredients. Pour into a well buttered 8" or 9" (20cm or 23 cm) pan. Refrigerate until set. Cut into squares.

VE Dark or **Milk Chocolate**
VE Vanilla Extract

5. Cocoa Fudge

Makes 8" (20 cm) pan

2 cups sugar	**500 ml**
2 Tbsp VE Pure Cocoa	**30 ml**
pinch salt	**pinch**
1 Tbsp butter	**15 ml**
1 cup milk	**250 ml**
1 tsp VE Vanilla Extract	**5 ml**

1. Whisk together, sugar, VE Pure Cocoa and salt. Add milk and butter, bring to a boil and cook for 15 minutes until mixture reaches soft ball stage (234°F - 112°C) reading on a candy thermometer.
2. Remove from heat, add VE Vanilla Extract, cool for 3 minutes. Beat fudge with a wooden spoon until it begins to stiffen. Pour into prepared pan. Refrigerate until set. Cut into squares.

VE Pure Cocoa & **VE Vanilla Extract**

6. Chocolate Hazelnut Clusters

1 lb VE Dark or Milk Chocolate, melted	**500 g**
1 cup toasted hazelnuts	**250 ml**

1. Toast hazelnuts on parchment lined bun pan at 350°F (175°C) for 15 minutes or until golden. Cool to room temperature.
2. Melt chocolate as directed. (See Successfully Melting Chocolate page 10). Add toasted hazelnuts and drop by teaspoon full on parchment lined bun pan. For a more decorative touch, you may drizzle the finished clusters with additional melted chocolate.

VE Dark or Milk Chocolate

Beverages - Hot and Cold

1. VE Cinnamon - Nutmeg Hot Chocolate
2. Freshly Brewed Mexican Coffee
3. Frosted Mocha
4. Classic Chocolate Shake
5. Chocolate Coffee Cooler
6. Banana Cocoa Smoothie
7. White Hot Chocolate with Almond
8. Minted Hot Chocolate

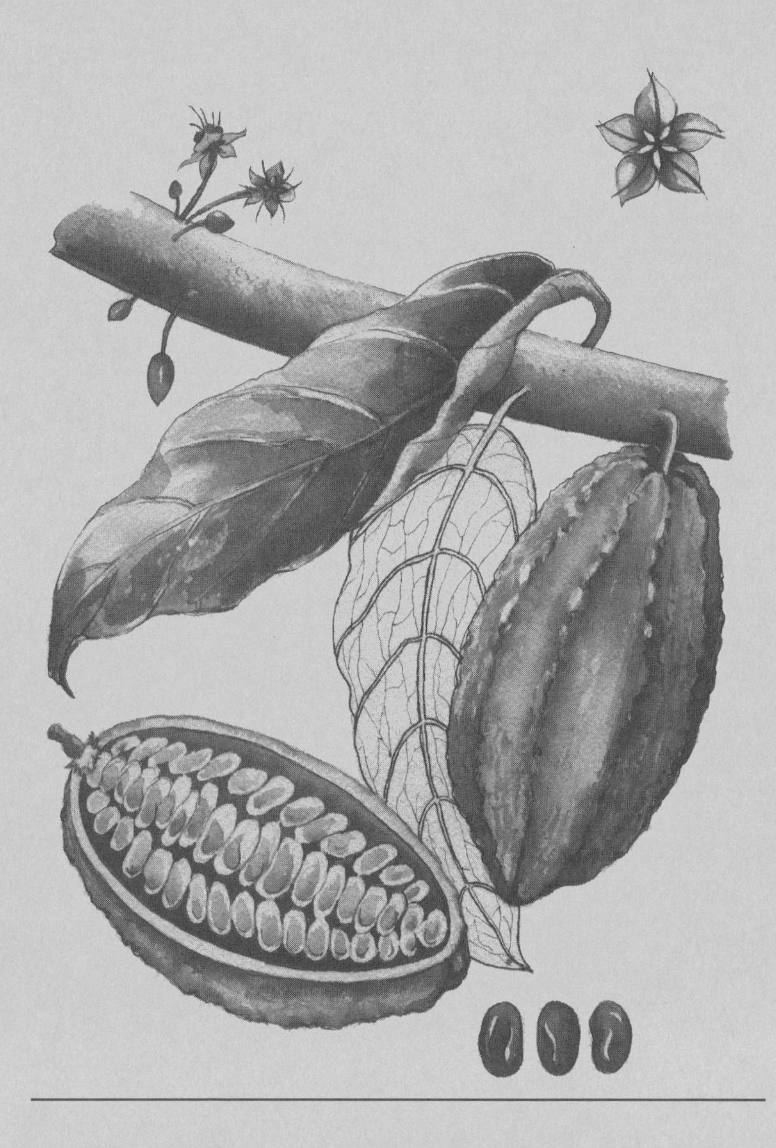

1. VE Cinnamon - Nutmeg Hot Chocolate

Serves 4

4 cups skim milk	**1 L**
1/4 cup VE Pure Cocoa	**60 ml**
1/4 cup sugar	**60 ml**
3/4 tsp VE Cinnamon	**3.75 ml**
1/4 tsp VE Nutmeg	**1.25 ml**
1/8 tsp VE Almond Extract	**0.6 ml**

1. In medium saucepan, whisk together VE Pure Cocoa, sugar, VE Cinnamon and VE Nutmeg.
2. Slowly add skim milk, stirring to make a smooth mixture. Add VE Almond Extract.
3. Heat over medium high heat until mixture is heated through. Whisk to make a foamy hot chocolate (or use our VE Froth Master)

Please note that this is a non-fat hot chocolate and according to the American Heart Association each cup has 149 calories and only 1 gram of fat.

VE Pure Cocoa
VE Cinnamon
VE Nutmeg
VE Almond Extract

2. Freshly Brewed Mexican Coffee

8 servings

1. For an 8 cup (2 L) pot of coffee, add 1/4 cup (60 ml) **VE Pure Cocoa** and 1/2 tsp (2.5 ml) ground **VE Cinnamon**.
2. Serve slightly sweetened and add cream if desired.

VE Pure Cocoa & **VE Cinnamon**.

3. Frosted Mocha

Serves 4

2 cups freshly brewed coffee, chilled	**500 ml**
6 Tbsp Chocolate Syrup (see recipe on page 65)	**90 ml**
2 cups vanilla ice cream, softened	**500 ml**
ice cubes made from coffee	

1. Place coffee, chocolate syrup and softened ice cream in blender. Blend until very smooth.
2. Spoon into tall glasses over frozen coffee ice cubes.

Chocolate Syrup (see recipe on page 65)

4. Classic Chocolate Shake

Serves 1

2 heaping scoops chocolate ice cream	**2 scoops**
3/4 cup milk, chilled	**180 ml**
1/3 cup VE Chocolate Syrup (see recipe page 65)	**80 ml**

1. Place ice cream, chilled milk and VE Chocolate Syrup in blender. Blend until smooth.
2. Pour into chilled glass, reserving any extra for a refill.

VE Chocolate Syrup (see recipe page 65)

5. Chocolate Coffee Cooler

Serves 6

1/4 cup VE Belgian Dark or Milk Chocolate	**60 ml**
1 cup strong, hot coffee	**250 ml**
3 cups milk	**750 ml**
4 cups chocolate or coffee ice cream	**1 L**

1. Place VE Belgian Chocolate in medium mixing bowl. Pour freshly brewed coffee over chocolate and stir with a wooden spoon until all chocolate is melted.
2. Slowly whisk in milk.
3. Combine chocolate mixture with ice cream, blend well. Serve immediately in tall, frosted glasses.

VE Belgian Dark or **Milk Chocolate**

6. Banana Cocoa Smoothie

Makes 2 cups (500 ml)

2 medium bananas, cut into 3 pieces	**2**
2 Tbsp VE Pure Cocoa	**30 ml**
1 Tbsp sugar or honey, or to taste	**15 ml**
1 cup milk, yogurt or orange juice	**250 ml**

1. Combine bananas, VE Pure Cocoa and honey (or sugar) in blender or food processor. Blend until smooth.
2. Add milk, yogurt or orange juice and process until smooth and frothy. Serve immediately in chilled glasses.

VE Pure Cocoa

7. White Hot Chocolate with Almond

Serves 4

4 cups milk	**1 L**
1/3 cup VE Belgian White Chocolate	**80 ml**
1/4 tsp VE Almond Extract	**1.25 ml**

1. Heat milk in large saucepan until scalding hot.
2. Add VE Belgian White Chocolate, stirring continuously until melted. Add VE Almond Extract. Serve in a mug, top with a little whipped cream, a dusting of **VE Pure Cocoa** and a **VE Cinnamon Stick** for stirring.

VE Belgian White Chocolate & VE Almond Extract
VE Pure Cocoa & VE Cinnamon Stick

8. Minted Hot Chocolate

Serves 4

4 cups milk	**1 L**
1/3 cup VE Pure Cocoa	**80 ml**
1/4 cup sugar	**60 ml**
1/4 tsp VE Peppermint Extract	**1.25 ml**

1. Whisk together VE Pure Cocoa and sugar. Add 1/2 cup (125 ml) cold milk and make a thin paste.
2. Heat remaining milk to scalding. Whisk 1 cup (250 ml) hot milk into cocoa paste, then add to heated milk. Stir in VE Peppermint Extract. Pour into mugs and serve.

Note: For an added touch, froth 1 cup (250 ml) cold milk in Frothmaster and divide between the mugs of hot chocolate. At holiday time use a candy canes for stir sticks.

VE Pure Cocoa
VE Peppermint Extract

9. Chocolate Coffee

Serves 1

1 cup strong, hot coffee	**250 ml**
2 Tbsp Chocolate Syrup (see recipe page 65)	**30 ml**
Whipped Cream	

1. Add Chocolate Syrup to hot coffee. Top with whipped cream. Dust with **VE Pure Cocoa**.

Chocolate Syrup (see recipe page 65)

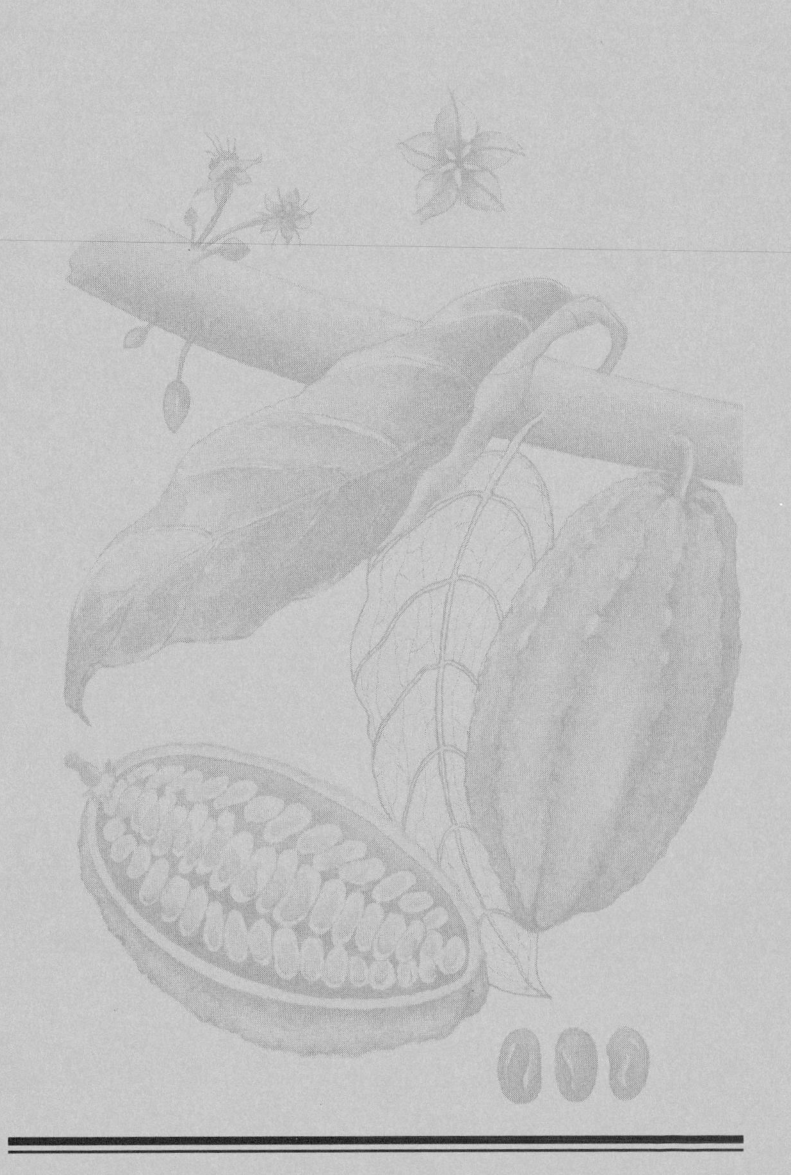

INDEX

Are You Looking for a Flexible and Creative Way to Earn an Income?

Create your own Epicure Selections business and enjoy...

- financial independence
- flexible hours, part time or full time
- the income you desire
- being your own boss
- incentives & bonuses
- learning new skills
- setting your own goals
- networking
- making new friends and contacts

Call your independent Epicure Selections Consultant to learn more and find out how to get your Sample Kit for Free!

To contact us:

Victorian Epicure Inc. / Epicure Selections
Tel: (250) 385-6563
Fax: (250) 385-4558
Box 5700
Victoria, British Colombia
V8R 6S8
E-Mail: hq@epicureselections.com
Web Site: www.epicureselections.com